Written by Claire Daniel

Illustrated by Pat Binder

STECK-VAUGHN
ELEMENTARY · SECONDARY · ADULT · LIBRARY

A Harcourt Classroom Education Company

www.steck-vaughn.com

Contents

ERA	PERIOD
Cenozoic	Quaternary
	Tertiary
Mesozoic	Cretaceous
	Jurassic
	Triassic
Paleozoic	Permian
	Carboniferous
	Devonian

CHAPTER 1

A Good Question

"Listen, everyone," Mrs. Fry said to her class. "We have one hour to study fossils here in the Interactive Science Museum. You and your partner will have one question to answer before we leave."

Alli couldn't believe her luck. Mrs. Fry had picked Robert to be her partner for the field trip to the museum. Robert knew all about fossils.

"How do we find the answer to our question?" Alli asked Mrs. Fry.

"The answers are in the museum. Look at the fossil displays and the signs beneath them," Mrs. Fry said. "You've never been to a museum like the Interactive Science Museum. It's really special. Just follow the directions at each interactive exhibit."

"What is *interactive*?" asked Robert.

"*Interactive* means that you get to do things with some of the exhibits, such as touching, smelling, or moving things," said Mrs. Fry.

Mrs. Fry handed a question out to each student pair. Alli and Robert's question said, *"Was it possible for a Tyrannosaurus rex to kill and eat a Stegosaurus?"*

Stegosaurus
[STEG-uh-SAWR-us]

Compsognathus
[komp-sug-NAY-thus]

Alli looked at Robert and asked, "Do you know the answer?"

"No, but let's start looking," answered Robert.

Robert and Alli walked toward all the fossil displays. They saw fossils of fish, ferns, leaves, dragonflies, shells, salamanders, shrimp, mollusks, and even a tree stump.

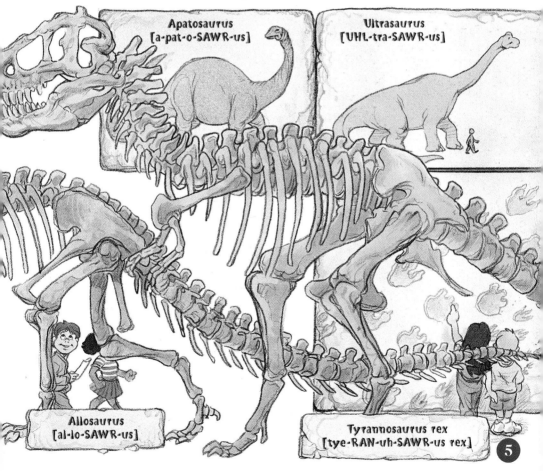

Apatosaurus
[a-pat-o-SAWR-us]

Ultrasaurus
[UHL-tra-SAWR-us]

Allosaurus
[al-lo-SAWR-us]

Tyrannosaurus rex
[tye-RAN-uh-SAWR-us rex]

Robert leaned closer to look at a fish fossil. "I have a fossil like this," he said. "My uncle gave it to me. He found it on his ranch in Oklahoma. He found dinosaur bones there, too."

"So do you think the answer to our question is here?" Alli asked.

"Maybe," answered Robert.

"What do you mean?" asked Alli.

"Well, I'm not really sure that the answer to our question is here," said Robert.

Alli was puzzled. "I thought you knew a lot about fossils...because of your uncle. And I always see you reading books about dinosaurs and fossils."

Robert smiled. "There's a lot I don't know. Uncle Paul got me interested in fossils when I spent the summer with him. He says that fossils tell us stories about the past."

"Fossils can't talk," Alli said.

Laughing, Robert walked over to look at a large fossil of a tree stump. "Scientists learn about plants and animals that lived millions of years ago by studying their fossils. That's how fossils tell stories."

"Let's go look at the dinosaurs," Alli said, staring at the dinosaur skeletons that towered above them. "These fossils are interesting, but dinosaurs are cool. Besides, I already know the answer to the question."

"You do? What is it?" Robert asked.

"Since Tyrannosaurus rex was the biggest dinosaur of all," Alli said, "it could've easily killed a Stegosaurus."

Robert pointed to a sign below a display of two large dinosaur leg bones. "But this sign says that the Ultrasaurus was the largest dinosaur."

"Ultrasaurus may have been bigger," Alli said. "But I still say Tyrannosaurus rex would've eaten Stegosaurus for lunch. Tyrannosaurus rex was probably faster and bigger and had razor-sharp teeth."

"You might be right," Robert said. "Let's see what stories the other dinosaur fossils tell us."

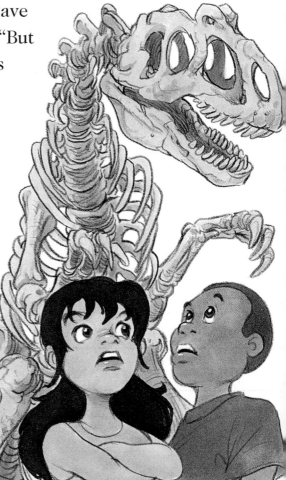

CHAPTER 2

Fossils Alive!

Alli pointed to a booth on the far side of the exhibit. A big sign above the booth was flashing brightly.

"Hey, that looks just like the photo booth at the mall," Alli said. "You know, the one that takes your picture."

"Yeah, except this one has a glass door," Robert said. "I bet it has pictures of different kinds of fossils inside instead of pictures of people."

"Well, I think we should go in and find out," Alli said.

Robert and Alli walked closer to the booth and peered through the glass.

Then they opened the booth's door and sat down inside. It was just big enough for two people. They faced a computer screen. A remote control lay beside the screen on a small shelf. A red button on the remote glowed.

Alli picked up the remote. "Let's see what happens," she said as she pushed the button.

The computer screen brightened with the image of a small dinosaur skeleton. A computer voice said, "This dinosaur was only about the size of a chicken. It lived about 180 to 200 million years ago, during the Jurassic Period. The fossil bones you see here were found in France."

The remote control beeped and another red button glowed. Alli pushed it.

Alli and Robert watched as the bones seemed to fill out and skin covered the dinosaur's body. Then the image of the dinosaur walked across the screen as if it were alive.

"Wow! It looks real!" said Alli. "How do scientists know what it looked like?"

The computer voice said, "Scientists study the fossils and put the bones together to make a skeleton. Then they compare it to animals living today. Scientists use what they know about animals today to discover how the dinosaur must have moved and looked."

Then the remote beeped again and a green button lit up. Alli pushed the button.

Once again the remote beeped, but this time three buttons lit up. They named three different time periods.

"Push Jurassic," Robert said. "I think that's when the Stegosaurus was alive."

Alli pushed it. Suddenly the booth started shaking, almost knocking them out of their seat. Smoke filled the booth, blocking the light from the glass door. They both shrieked as red and green lights flashed and blinked. Robert pushed against the door.

Then everything stopped. Robert and Alli looked around in the booth's smoky darkness.

"What happened?" Robert asked nervously.

Alli's heart was pounding. "I think the booth broke. Let's get out of here," she said.

CHAPTER 3

Where Are We?

Robert pushed against the door. It slowly swung open. The partners peered out of the booth. There was no class, no Mrs. Fry, and no museum in sight.

"What's going on?" Alli asked. "Where in the world are we?"

"I don't know," Robert said, blinking his eyes. "But look at this place. It's beautiful!"

Large, white clouds floated in the vast blue sky. Lush, green ferns surrounded them, while palm trees towered above them. Bright sunshine warmed their faces.

Alli turned around and saw a waterfall of clear, blue water. It poured into a stream of water that disappeared into the dense cover of ferns and palm trees. Dragonflies flew in the warm air, then flitted down and rested on the top of the slowly moving stream. A gentle breeze blew in the air.

"Wow!" Robert said slowly. "Look at all the insects. They're everywhere!"

Alli turned again and saw a mountain in the distance. A smoky trail floated up in the sky from its top. "Is that a volcano?" she asked.

"I think so," Robert said.

"This place is really cool-looking. But I haven't seen any signs of people, houses, or cars," Alli said. "It's almost like we've traveled back in time."

"It doesn't seem possible," said Robert, "but I think you might be right. Remember the Jurassic button you pushed? Maybe we're in the Jurassic Period!"

"No way—" Alli stopped talking, then shook her head. "That's crazy!"

"Look," said Robert. "See these leaves? They look like ferns. The museum had fossils of leaves that looked just like this."

"I remember them!" Alli exclaimed. "And look at this salamander! I remember seeing a fossil that looked just like it."

"Remember the dragonfly fossils?" Robert asked, his voice rising in excitement.

Alli thought for a moment and said, "Wait a minute. You can find dragonflies, ferns, and salamanders in any warm place."

"Yes," said Robert. "But right now there aren't any volcanoes back home."

"You mean there aren't any *active* volcanoes back home," Alli reminded Robert.

"You're right about that," said Robert, looking at the mountain's smoky top.

Then Alli said, "I still want to know where we are and *when* we are."

The remote control beeped, and a red button glowed. "I think the remote is trying to tell us something," said Robert.

Alli pushed the red button. A computer voice said, "You are now in the Jurassic Period." Robert and Alli looked at each other in surprise.

CHAPTER 4

Searching for Dinosaurs

"Is this what Mrs. Fry meant when she said we'd never been to a museum like *this* before?" Robert asked.

"I don't know, but I've never interacted with science like this," Alli said. "Now what do we do?"

"We need to look for clues to answer our question," Robert said. "Let's follow this stream. Water attracts all sorts of animals."

"Animals? What kind?" Alli asked.

"Dinosaurs, of course!" said Robert as he jumped over the stream and ran into the brush.

"What dinosaurs?" Alli asked as she followed Robert.

Robert crouched beside a fallen tree on the forest floor. It was partly covered with mud.

"This tree trunk," he said, "looks like the one we saw in the museum!"

The remote beeped, and a red button flashed. Alli pushed it.

The computer voice explained, "A dead tree can become a fossil when it is covered by mud and sand. Rain falls, and the water seeps through the mud into the decaying tree, filling the empty pockets of air. The water evaporates, but the minerals stay in the tree. After many years, the minerals get hard. Millions of years later, it becomes a rock. That rock is really a fossil!"

Alli pointed to a large footprint and said, "Whoa! What's this?"

The same button on the remote flashed. She pushed it again.

"This will be a different kind of fossil," the voice said. "An animal walks by and makes a track like this. Then mud covers the footprint and makes a cast. When the print hardens into stone, it has become a fossil. After millions of years, somebody digs up the fossil."

"That's not what I meant," she said. "What—or who—made the footprint?"

The remote button flashed again, and the computer voice answered, "That footprint was made by an Apatosaurus."

Suddenly a loud noise, sounding like a deep horn, shattered the stillness. Startled, Robert and Alli jerked their heads in the direction of the noise. They both gasped.

In the distance, a huge creature bellowed and moved.

A dinosaur!

It was as long as six cars put together end-to-end. The dinosaur slowly raised its head to eat the leaves on the very top branches of a tree.

The remote flashed, and the voice said, "In the distance you see a live Apatosaurus. Fossil remains of Apatosaurus bones have been found in Colorado, Oklahoma, Utah, and Wyoming."

"It's huge!" Robert exclaimed. "It's bigger than a dozen elephants!"

"Do you think it's dangerous?" Alli said, sounding worried.

The remote beeped, and the button flashed. "No. The Apatosaurus only eats plants," the computer voice said. "The only danger is if it steps on you by mistake."

"You know what? We can stay here," Alli said, "and watch for the mighty Tyrannosaurus rex to come and eat it for lunch."

"That could never happen," the computer voice said. "The Tyrannosaurus rex lived much later, in a totally different time period. But another kind of dinosaur, such as an Allosaurus, might come along and kill it."

"Let's step closer and get a better look," Robert suggested.

As Robert and Alli pushed through the brush, they saw a nest of large eggs. "Ooh! Look at these," Robert said. "I hope these eggs don't belong to the Apatosaurus. I wonder if they'll ever become fossils."

The remote beeped. "If the eggs get covered with sand or mud, they could someday become fossils the same way the tree stump did," the voice said. "The eggs lie underground for millions of years. During this time a lot of rain falls. The mineral-filled water soaks into the ground. The water seeps into tiny holes in the eggs. The water evaporates, but the minerals stay in the eggs, making them hard. The eggs turn to stone as they become fossils!"

"So that's the way dinosaur bones become fossils, too?" Alli asked.

"Exactly!" said the computer voice.

Alli pushed aside a huge palm leaf. She gasped for breath at what she saw. "What's that?" she whispered.

Not far in front of her stood a pointy-faced dinosaur with large, trunk-like legs. Eighteen bony plates lined its back and spiked tail. With large jaws it tore off leaves. Its huge flat teeth chewed the delicious green meal. Then it ambled toward the stream for a drink.

"It's a Stegosaurus!" Robert whispered.

The remote lit up and commented, "You're right. The Stegosaurus also lived in the Jurassic Period. Scientists have found Stegosaurus bones in Colorado, Oklahoma, Utah, and Wyoming."

Suddenly the ground shook beneath Alli and Robert. It was as if a cement truck had legs and was jumping up and down.

THRUM! THRUM! THRUM!

Alli grabbed Robert's arm and looked around wildly. "Do you feel that? Where's it coming from?"

"I don't know," Robert said, "but it sounds like something big is headed our way."

Alli nodded. "And it's coming fast!"

CHAPTER 5

A Narrow Escape

"Quick!" Alli yelled. "Get up on that rock and see what it is."

Robert climbed to the top. "It's huge! Taller than a tree!"

"Another Apatosaurus?" Alli guessed.

"No," Robert said. "It's walking on its hind legs and has a head that bobs like a chicken.

It's got a thick tail that's wagging, but it sure doesn't look friendly." He shuddered. "And take a look at those huge teeth, too!"

The remote beeped, and the computer said, "That is an Allosaurus. It's hungry and looking for its next meal. It may go after either the Apatosaurus or the Stegosaurus."

Robert exclaimed, "The Allosaurus is going after the Stegosaurus. And we're in its path!"

"Run!" Alli yelled. "Before WE become fossils ourselves!"

They ran back the way they had come, weaving through the thick ferns and following the stream. The Allosaurus was right behind them!

Then Robert and Alli waded into the stream. They slipped under the waterfall and crouched behind the wall of water. Seconds later they watched the huge Allosaurus thunder past them, crushing everything in its path.

"Want to make a run for it?" Robert asked. The booth was just across the stream.

Then they heard the booming footsteps of a second Allosaurus following the first. The booth was directly in its path!

"We've got to reach the booth before the second dinosaur crushes it!" Robert cried. "It's our only way out of here!"

They bolted across the stream and ran inside
the dark booth, banging the door shut. The
yellow button on the remote glowed.

RETURN TO MUSEUM

CHAPTER 6

A Question Answered

Roaring, the Allosaurus knocked the booth on its side. Alli and Robert fell into a heap, and the remote dropped beside them.

Robert quickly grabbed the remote and pushed the yellow button. As the dinosaur roared again, red and green lights began flashing. Smoke filled the booth while it shook and rattled. The booth was knocked upside-down and then back up again.

Suddenly everything was quiet. A green button glowed on the remote.

FOSSILS ALIVE!

Alli and Robert breathed a sigh of relief. "Should I push it?" Robert joked. "We can visit a different time period. Maybe we'd see what Tyrannosaurus rex likes for lunch."

Alli yelled, "No way! That's all the science I want to interact with for now."

Alli and Robert pushed against the booth door. But it wouldn't open. "We have to push harder," Robert said. "Ready, one…two…THREE!"

Alli and Robert pushed as hard as they could. Finally the booth door swung open. Alli and Robert stumbled through the doorway. Then they stopped.

There stood their class right by the fossil exhibit, as if nothing had ever happened. Robert and Alli looked at each other, caught their breath, then joined their classmates.

Mrs. Fry asked the class, "Do any pairs have the answer to their question?"

Robert and Alli winked at each other. Robert said, "Mrs. Fry, we can answer our question now."

Mrs. Fry smiled and asked, "Well, was it possible for a Tyrannosaurus rex to kill and eat a Stegosaurus?"

"No," Alli said. "The Tyrannosaurus rex and the Stegosaurus lived in completely different time periods, millions of years apart."

"Excellent!" said Mrs. Fry. "How did you two discover this information?"

"We interacted with science," said Robert, "and the fossils told us everything!"